DATE DUE

DEC 15 1975		
FEB 3 1976		
APR 15 1976		
MAY 11	DE 1 3 '00	
NOV 2 1976		
MAY 29 1979	DE 08 '03	
APR 1 1980	OC 28 '04	
SEP 2 1980		
AUG. 8 1984		
MY 1 '85		
MR 2 5 '88		
MY 0 3 '88		
JE 0 9 '88		
NO 2 1 '88		

HIGHSMITH 45-102   PRINTED IN U.

W9-AKB-210

3
973.3   11,697
Hi   Hirsch, S. Carl
          Famous American Revolutionary war heroes.
        Line drawings by Lorence Bjorklund.   Chicago,
        Rand McNally, 1974
          [95]p.   illus.

          1.U.S.-History-Revolution, 1775-1783-
        Biography.   I.Bjorklund, Lorence, illus.
        II.Title.

EAU CLAIRE DISTRICT LIBRARY

Famous American Revolutionary War Heroes

FAMOUS AMERICAN REVOLUTIONARY WAR HEROES is an exciting narrative of the thirteen colonies' eight-year struggle for freedom. Award-winning author S. Carl Hirsch weaves a colorful tapestry of the revolutionary period from the Boston Massacre right up through the Battle of Yorktown. Vividly he describes key events—the Boston Tea Party, the Battle of Bunker Hill, the winter at Valley Forge—and delves into the character of the people central to them. And throughout—whether describing the lauded General George Washington or the little-known Sergeant Joseph Plumb Martin—he focuses on one vital issue. What was it that inspired them? What commitment to a lofty ideal led these ordinary, everyday people to heroism? How could young Nathan Hale face death so nobly? From what hidden wellsprings of courage did Abigail Adams draw her strength and energy? What prompted John Paul Jones's reckless courage?

Sensitively and with great insight, author Hirsch probes these and other questions, concluding that the "war's outcome was not to be decided by any of the usual explanations—overwhelming manpower, superior firepower, greater wealth, better supplies, abler commanders. Instead, some fateful and hidden factor would determine the war's conclusion, the spirit of men and women fighting for freedom."

An inspiring book, FAMOUS AMERICAN REVOLUTIONARY WAR HEROES is richly illustrated with full-color reproductions of famous paintings of the revolutionary war scene, including the works of artists such as Emanuel Leutze

Continued on inside of back cover

CANADA

L. SUPERIOR

L. HURON

MICHIGAN

L. MICHIGAN

L. ERIE

L. ONTARIO

WISCONSIN

ILLINOIS

INDIANA

OHIO

Vincennes

Ohio River

Kaskaskia

KENTUCKY

TENNESSEE

MISSISSIPPI

ALABAMA

GEORGIA

FLORIDA

GULF OF MEXICO

NEW YORK

Saratoga

Hudson River

VT. MAINE

N.H.

MASS.
CONN.

R.I.

Lexington
Bunker Hill

White Plains

Delaware R.

Princeton

Manhattan

Long Island
Trenton
Monmouth

Valley Forge

PENNSYLVANIA

MD.

DEL.

Philadelphia

WEST
VIRGINIA

Yorktown *

VIRGINIA

Chesapeake
Bay

NORTH CAROLINA

SOUTH
CAROLINA

ATLANTIC OCEAN

WITHDRAWN

LEGEND

——— Original 13 Colonies'
Prewar Boundary *

★ Battle Sites

* Note: The original 13 colonies
are labeled in blue. Other states
indicated on the map are for
present-day orientation.

Famous American Revolutionary War Heroes

Famous American Revolutionary War Heroes

By S. CARL HIRSCH

Line Drawings by LORENCE BJORKLUND

RAND MᶜNALLY & COMPANY · CHICAGO · NEW YORK · SAN FRANCISCO

EAU CLAIRE DISTRICT LIBRARY

82014

11,697

Library of Congress Cataloging in Publication Data

Hirsch, S. Carl.
    FAMOUS AMERICAN REVOLUTIONARY WAR HEROES.

SUMMARY: From the Boston Massacre through the Battle
of Yorktown, traces the wartime activities of eight Revolu-
tionary War heroes central to the American cause.
    1. United States—History—Revolution, 1775–1783—Bi-
ography—Juvenile literature. [1. United States—History—
Revolution, 1775–1783—Biography] 1. Bjorklund, Lorence
F., illus. II. Title.
E206.H57   973.3'092'2 [B] [920]   74-8469
ISBN 0-528-82467-8
ISBN 0-528-82468-6 (lib. bdg.)

Copyright © 1974 by RAND McNALLY & COMPANY

All rights reserved

Printed in the United States of America
by RAND McNALLY & COMPANY

First printing, 1974

Book Design by
MARIO PAGLIAI

FRONT COVER:
Detail from *Washington at the Battle
of Monmouth Heights, June, 1778*
by Emanuel Leutze
KIRBY COLLECTION, LAFAYETTE COLLEGE
EASTON, PENNSYLVANIA

Contents

A Time for Valor

THIS WAS THE strangest of wars. The American Revolution was not expected to last eight months—let alone eight years.

It began almost haphazardly, without a master plan on either side. The watching world could hardly have guessed at any moment of the conflict which side would finally show the white flag of surrender.

The war's outcome was not to be decided by any of the usual explanations—overwhelming manpower, superior firepower, greater wealth, better supplies, abler commanders. Instead, some fateful and hidden factor would determine the war's conclusion, the spirit of men and women fighting for freedom.

In the raw, blustery winter months of early 1770, there was bloodshed in Boston. An eleven-year-old boy, Christopher Seider, was killed by a petty British official, an informer who spied on rebels. Eleven days later came the Boston Massacre, in which five Americans died by the gunfire of British redcoats, confused and beset by an angry crowd.

Violence set into motion its own chain of counterblows and revenge, punishment and defiance. Facts and rumors passed quickly from Boston to Baltimore, from Philadelphia to Savannah, and out into the dark frontier. There were wrathful mutterings in this land about unfair British taxes, crown regulations as to what and where Americans could buy and

11

OPPOSITE PAGE:
Drafting of the Declaration of Independence
by J. L. G. Ferris
COURTESY OF LONGINES-WITTNAUER, INC.

sell, restrictions on the rights of the colonies to govern themselves.

Even in both houses of the British Parliament there were those who said that King George III and his ministers were carrying things too far. In the House of Commons, one member of Parliament cried out: "I rejoice that America has resisted!"

One after the other, the American colonies defied British taxes and stopped buying British goods. In England, thousands of grim and jobless workmen were turned out into the streets because Americans refused to accept imports from Britain.

Tension rose in the colonies and in the mother country. A dispute in angry words was giving way to a conflict of open deeds. The colonists staged a few audacious acts of resistance. But this was not rebellion. Hardly a single voice was calling for the overthrow of imperial rule. As yet, this was still British America, and its people demanded only "the full rights of Englishmen."

In the stormy years that followed, a segment of America's two million people took an active part in the struggle. Among them were those in whom the idea of Liberty burned like an abiding flame. But they were ordinary, everyday people who had no thought of becoming heroes and heroines. Who can say what part their personal courage played in the conflict between a "rabble in arms" and the world's most formidable land and sea power?

Son of Liberty

RISING EARLY, Samuel Adams walked swiftly to the dock in Boston Bay to make sure the three ships were still there. In the morning mist they lay like a trio of ghosts at Griffin's Wharf. Townsmen were standing watch around the clock, and they gave Adams a cheery greeting.

The *Dartmouth, Beaver,* and *Eleanor* rode low in the water. In their holds was a British cargo more explosive than gunpowder. The ships were full of tea, a commodity bearing a royal tax which American rebels had vowed never to pay.

Samuel Adams marveled at how quickly his fellow colonists had abandoned a lifelong tea-drinking custom. Tea had become for them not only a symbol of British tyranny. Many had also persuaded themselves that the stuff was poisonous, fattening, and brought on early baldness!

But tea was only one of the many British products that were being shunned by the Americans. From Georgia to Massachusetts, there was a growing mood of resistance to British high-handedness. Many of the colonists had decided to show the mother country they could do without her goods.

The American buyers' ban had become a vexing problem to King George III and his Parliament. Never in their long years of imperial rule had the British suffered such open defiance from their colonies.

13

OVERLEAF:
*Pulling Down the Statue of
George III, New York, 1776*
by William Walcutt
FROM THE COLLECTION OF
GILBERT DARLINGTON

An imperial pattern had been jointly established by that handful of small European nations which ruled over vast areas of Asia, Africa and the Americas. Colonies were looked upon as a cheap source of raw materials. Too, colonies were to serve as a profitable market for goods from the mother country. Now, in America, Britain was trying to impose still another burden: the colonies were to be used as a direct source of tax revenue. With the duty on tea, Britain was testing its power to levy taxes on the colonists. The issue was deadlocked on the Boston docks where three tea ships had been tied up unloaded for nineteen days.

While all the colonies were involved in the tea-tax dispute, the situation in Boston was especially tense because the authority of the crown in Boston was backed up by a military force of British regulars. But Adams was more concerned this day about turncoats than redcoats. Each of the American colonies had its share of the "king's men," royalists with a pious faith in the British crown. It was said that they had "their bodies in America and their hearts in England." These Tories held positions of power in Boston, and their agents were everywhere.

Adams moved warily among them. On this day, December 16, 1773, Boston rebels under his leadership would stage their most daring act of resistance against Tory rule. And Samuel planned the day's errands with care. It was Thursday, a market day, and he spent part of his morning among the stalls. He noted with satisfaction that there were few British wares being bought. Well-acquainted with the politics of everyone in town, he stopped to chat with townsfolk, reminding them of an important meeting to be held later that morning.

By ten o'clock, Samuel found himself in the pulpit of the Old South Meetinghouse. A thousand or more Boston citizens had gathered to hear the latest report on the tea ships. Adams ran the meeting skillfully. Committees were dispatched to make a last effort at returning the "despised cargo" to Britain, and the meeting was recessed until reports could be made.

At the Green Dragon Tavern, Adams stopped for a noontime meeting with a group of friends who called themselves "Mohawks." These were a dependable group of Yankee rebels, well-prepared for their part in the events scheduled for later that day. One of the townsmen had composed a little song for the occasion, and he delighted Adams with a verse or two: "Rally, Mohawks! Bring out your axes, and tell King George we'll pay no taxes!"

By 5:45 P.M. Adams was back in the pulpit of the Old South Meetinghouse. A huge crowd overflowed the church. As the candles were being lit, he looked out into the glow of several thousand faces.

Samuel was no spellbinder. He spoke plainly in a high, thin voice. And he indulged in no lofty or stirring oratory. Every reasonable step had now been taken, he said, to get the unwanted cargo returned to England. It was clear that the demands of the Boston colonists were being ignored and defied. He whacked his gavel. "This meeting can do nothing further to *save the country*."

The last three words touched off a deafening echo throughout the hall. "Save the country!" It was as though a signal had been sounded; cheer after cheer rang out and the crowd poured into the streets.

In the midst of the throng were several hundred "Mohawks," ludicrously garbed, make-believe Indians. Their faces were smeared with lampblack and ash. Some wore blankets and headbands. All carried hatchets or sledges.

It was now nightfall. The crowds streamed toward the docks. There the tea ships were quickly boarded in the half-light of torches and lanterns. To the sound of mock Indian war whoops, the "Mohawks" set to work hauling the chests of teas up from the ships' holds by winch and tackle.

There was bedlam as the crowds lining the docks shouted their encouragement while the raiders smashed the tea chests into splinters. Two thousand chests, each containing 320 pounds of choice British tea, were dumped into the icy waters of Boston Harbor.

Announcing nine o'clock, the town crier sounded his "All's well!" The crowd gave him a hearty cheer and headed for their homes. The party was over. There was no damage to any of the ships, and a single broken padlock was to be quietly replaced the next day.

Samuel Adams went home to share a cup of hot milk with his good wife, Betsy. The Boston patriot chuckled to himself, reveling in the night's bold jest. But he spent little time congratulating himself on the success of the "tea party." He was already planning his next move.

· · ·

Boston had brewed for Britain a bitter tea. George III reacted to the Boston Tea Party like a wrathful parent punishing a wayward child. In the weeks and months following, Parliament passed a series of what Bostonians called "Intolerable Acts." These were planned to teach the defiant town a harsh lesson. Britain clearly intended to bring Boston to its knees and to serve notice on any other impudent colony as well.

Until the dumped tea was paid for, the Intolerable Acts decreed, the port of Boston would remain closed. In addition, town meetings were banned. The people were deprived of their right to choose judges and juries. Boston was placed under a military governor, General Thomas Gage. Five regiments of British regulars were sent to occupy the town, and the royal fleet would blockade the harbor.

The busy docks of seagoing Boston were stilled. Seamen, dockhands, shipbuilders were out of work. Deep-sea fishing was halted. Through the spring and summer of 1774, this saltwater town and its imperial captors settled into a long, stubborn stalemate.

With Boston shackled and bound, Samuel Adams doubled his efforts. Skillfully he drew more and more Boston citizens to the rebel cause. He kept a list of men and women still uncommitted who might well serve the patriots' movement. And gradually he enlisted them with their talents, resources, and influence.

At age fifty-one, Samuel Adams was no callow dreamer playing at insurrection. His style of life was moderate, middling, modest. A strict Puritan, in battling tyranny he fervently believed he was best serving the Lord. If Samuel had any one single passion, it was for the common welfare of America. His personal needs were few. Since his early years he had had no private business. His father had been a well-to-do malt dealer, but Samuel had no talent for business and his fortunes went steadily downhill.

To some he was known as "the other Adams" in contrast to his more prosperous cousin John. Samuel's occupation was that of full-time rebel. But demanding as the job was, it paid nothing. So this Harvard-educated man from a good Boston family trudged the crooked streets of the town in a mended waistcoat, well-worn shoes, and a tricorn hat that had seen too many seasons. He was stubby, thick-chested, with a strong face and piercing blue eyes. Unstylish, he wore no wig. And his clothes appeared as though he had slept in them—if he had slept at all.

His fellow townsmen saw him as a plain, decent citizen, but hardly a hero. He utterly lacked the dashing warrior style or a flare for bluster. His trembling fingers would have made him a menace with firearms. And until this time, Samuel hadn't even learned to ride a horse!

But no one could question Samuel Adams's patriotic zeal or the depth of his commitment. He was certain that "the natural liberty of man is to be free from any superior power on earth." At a time when most of his fellow American patriots still believed in the divine right of kings, Adams affirmed the equal rights of all men.

Although Samuel knew that America was not yet ready to break with the British crown, he centered his main efforts on welding the unity of the colonies in defense of their own freedom. Stretched out along fifteen hundred miles of the Atlantic seaboard, the thirteen provinces were separated not only by distance; they were disunited as well by background and religion, by customs and competition, jealousy, and bigotry.

As Britain tightened its hold on the closed port of Boston, Adams cried out to the colonies for help. "Boston is now suffering in the common cause," he wrote in his letters. "The liberties of all alike are invaded by the same haughty power!"

The response was swift and strong. Overland came relief in food, clothing, and money. A flock of sheep was driven from Brooklyn, and another from Rhode Island. Barrels of fish were carted down from Salem and Marblehead. Cheese came from Pennsylvania, corn from Virginia, rice from the Carolinas.

Adams was now in touch with letter-writing committees in every colony, with Sons of Liberty active in the coastal cities, the New Hampshire uplands, the Delaware tidewater, the Kentucky backwoods, the southern Piedmont. Express riders brought heartening support from these "Committees of Correspondence."

The letter writing moved the colonies toward a fateful decision. By late summer the thirteen separate colonies agreed to come together in a Continental Congress, to be held in Philadelphia beginning September 5, 1774.

Samuel was, of course, elected as one of the four Massachusetts delegates to the historic Congress. With his election, a strange little pageant unfolded at the somewhat neglected Adams house on Purchase Street. One summer day, a tailor appeared to measure the bewildered Samuel for a new suit. Then came in order the wigmaker, hatter, cobbler. And finally he was sent a purse of spending money. Over his protests, fellow Bostonians explained to Adams that since he was to represent them in the Congress, they wanted him to be a proper delegate in every way.

At last, on an August morning, a fine coach-and-four appeared, well fitted-out for the trip to Philadelphia. Samuel emerged from his house resplendent in a wine-colored coat, ruffled linen, powdered wig, and silver-buckled shoes.

A crowd of townsfolk came to bid him an affectionate farewell. As one friend said, he admired Adams's courage to live as he did— "with his head inside the lion's mouth."

.   .   .

As ruler of a world-wide empire, England was long experienced in putting down all forms of colonial dissent. The British overlords well knew the difference between protest and sedition, between reform and revolution. In Samuel Adams, they saw a man who would be satisfied with nothing less than the overthrow of British rule in America.

Thus he was a marked man and no ordinary Son of Liberty. In the high councils of the British imperial government, Adams was singled out as probably the most dangerous individual in America. The king's ministers fluffed their wigs and tapped their snuffboxes as they pondered the evidence of high treason that might be brought against Adams.

In Boston, Samuel's fellow patriots warned him to watch his words lest they lose his services to the gallows. The most dangerous of these words was "independence." Samuel had learned in Philadelphia that his fellow delegates to the Continental Congress were uneasy at the very idea of separation from England. Most were of the opinion that the quarrel between the colonies and the mother country could somehow be patched up. A good many were unwilling to face the charge of treason.

Samuel Adams was no daredevil, but he refused to live in daily fear of arrest and he deftly sidestepped the dangling noose. A bulldog of a man, tough, fearless, tenacious, he carefully avoided unnecessary risks. He kept no telltale diary. Every revealing letter he received he scissored into shreds and threw to the winds. He wrote for the newspapers unceasingly, but hid behind a score of pen names. Shrewdly he planned the rebel tactics in Boston and kept a sharp eye on the opposition.

In the spring of 1775, the perplexed royal governor in Boston, General Gage, pondered his next move. Stealthy rebel movements all around him had set his nerves on edge. General Gage debated whether to lay hands on the rebel ringleaders, or seize the stores of arms which he knew were being secretly gathered outside of Boston.

At this time, the American colonists were making preparations for the Second Continental Congress. In Boston, the Sons of Liberty took steps to safeguard their delegates from arrest. Samuel Adams was sent into hiding in the nearby village of Lexington, along with delegate John Hancock.

Just before dawn, the steady tread of the British regulars could be heard approaching Lexington. Adams and John Hancock were already making their escape. On the far edge of town, they paused in a maple grove. From a distance came the sound of the gunfire that would later be called "the shot heard round the world."

In deep joy, Samuel Adams welcomed the rising sun of the new day. "Oh, what a glorious morning is this!" he cried out. "I mean for America."

OVERLEAF:
Paul Revere Crossing the Charles
by A. Lassell Ripley
COPYRIGHT: THE PAUL REVERE LIFE
INSURANCE COMPANY

A Woman of Courage

IN SPITE OF her dread of war, Abigail Adams knew that the undeclared conflict around Boston foreshadowed the real thing. "Did ever any kingdom or state regain its liberty when once it was invaded—without bloodshed?" she asked.

Brief months before, she had been a Boston housewife still in her twenties, married to attorney John Adams and the mother of four. Suddenly now, in the late autumn of 1774, she was a hard-working "farmeress" in the nearby village of Braintree, her husband absent. She had become one of the "war widows" of rebel Boston, women who were learning their own strength as patriots. As gentle Abigail wrote in mock boastfulness to her husband in Philadelphia, "If our men are drawn off and we should be attacked, you will find a race of Amazons in America!"

Gradually she undertook the full task of providing for her family. A preacher's daughter, Abigail was a delicate woman, with an elegance in her manner, in the fine arch of her brow, and in the grace of her walk. Yet she now farmed as strenuously as any man.

In November, 1774, her first harvest was in—grain and fruit, potatoes and beans. Hams hung in the smokehouse, and her own flour was back from the miller. There was feed for the livestock, dried flax to be woven, and rendered fat for soap making. Abigail felt a glow of pride.

Each day she held classes for her own children, and they were better taught than they had ever been in school. In addition, she found time to help others in distress, to lend some of her own new-found strength where it was needed. Gradually, the Adams's farmhouse in Braintree became a busy center of rebel activity.

In the arc of hills surrounding British-occupied Boston glowed the watch fires of the Yankees. Their strength gained and lost from day to day. Fresh recruits arrived. But other volunteers departed almost at will, since they had joined up for only brief periods and left whenever they were needed at home.

Often there were skirmishes between rebels and redcoats. Patriots in Boston and the surrounding countryside carried on constant sabotage and spying. Sons of Liberty were smuggled in and out of sealed Boston. Yankee munitions were gathered and stored. Guerrilla raids destroyed British supplies. Much of this secret activity was planned in Abigail Adams's parlor.

The British had their own network of paid spies, but they were no match for the intelligence network of the Americans. The rebels had a thousand eyes and ears that were alert around the clock. By a variety of wily methods, reports were transmitted to the rebel headquarters at Cambridge. Church bells ringing at odd hours, children delivering "nonsense" notes to their friends, petticoats arranged in a certain way on clotheslines, carters trundling firewood—all these were parts of the voluntary American spy organization.

Abigail had the additional task of funneling important information to the Continental Congress, meeting in Philadelphia. Almost daily she sent her husband warm-hearted letters that expressed her affection, her longing and loneliness. But between the words of endearment he received a complete report of what was happening on the critical Boston scene, the main colonial arena of conflict.

Mrs. Adams gave readily of her own energy and wisdom, just as she willingly turned over her fine pewter spoons to be made into musket balls. Her keen intelligence told her that she stood at a turning point in one of mankind's momentous struggles for freedom. And no sacrifice could be too great.

Her heart was torn by the young men who tramped past her farm on their way to take up arms under the Yankee banner. "Many, very many of our heroes," she wrote, "will spend their lives in the cause."

Her house was a way station, a crossroads, a hostel for the weary and distressed, a rendezvous for volunteers and partisans. Refugees from Boston stayed a day, a night, a week. Continental recruits stopped by for lodging or a meal. People were bedded down in the kitchen. Her own bedchamber and the children's rooms contained a vast number of cradles and cribs. The barn loft was like a barracks.

At times, Abigail was seized with migraine headaches that pounded her temples, set her retching, and turned her face ashen. But she simply pursed her lips into a thin, determined line, fastened an apron about her, and turned to the needs of others.

In the late spring of 1775, she did what she could to help prepare for one of the critical battles of the American Revolution. The risks ahead were great, considering the state of Yankee manpower, training, armaments.

"Courage I know we have in abundance," Abigail wrote to her husband, "but powder—where shall we get a sufficient supply?"

Characteristically, she supplied her own answer. In her barn in Braintree, Mrs. Adams began the dangerous work of manufacturing saltpeter, the basic ingredient of gunpowder.

.   .   .

At 4:00 A.M. on June 17, 1775, Abigail Adams was roused by what seemed to be thunder and earthquake, both at once. Hurriedly she woke eight-year-old Johnny. Together they climbed breathlessly to the crest of nearby Penn's Hill. Abigail put her eye to a long spyglass. In the predawn light, she could watch the cannonading which was to open the Battle of Bunker Hill.

Long months of wary waiting and preparation by the opposing British and American forces had suddenly ended with a bold move by the Yankees. Boston and Charlestown were built on two hilly knobs of land that faced each other across the Charles River. In the hot summer night of June 16, rebel troops had stealthily moved out on the Charlestown peninsula and mounted the dark hills.

With picks and shovels the men had begun digging fortifications. The main rebel stronghold was to crown a broad, sloping pasture. This was land once farmed by a man named Breed. But the battle fought here would be known for the heights owned by Farmer Bunker, just beyond. Less than half a mile across the river lay sleeping Boston, held by the redcoats.

Muffling sounds and working without light, the Americans dug, piled, tamped the earth. The rebels were more skilled with shovels and axes than with bayonets and cannons. Most were farmers who had often pounded their pickaxes into the stony New England soil. The night was sultry. The men, bare-chested and barefoot, labored hastily but steadily to construct an oblong earthwork called a redoubt. They knew well what lay ahead. Within hours they would be defending their own lives in this makeshift fort, which must be completed in the dark hours of a single night.

General William Howe, in command of His Majesty's troops, exploded in rage when he was awakened in the early morning hours of June 17. Aides directed his sleep-filled eyes to the new structure suddenly rising on the murky crest of Breed's Hill. British gunboats in the river had already begun arching cannonballs toward the rebel fort, with little effect. Howe ordered preparations for a river crossing and a full-scale attack on the rebel position.

From their hilltop, Abigail Adams and her son shaded their eyes from the bright sunlight and followed the action. Abigail pointed out to

Johnny the Yankee strengths and weaknesses, the things to watch for on the distant battle scene.

Mortars and ships' guns now began to bombard the Yankee positions on the hill. Cannonballs, the big twenty-four-pounders, thundered from barges in the river. Mother and son gazed in horror as abandoned Charlestown turned into an inferno, church steeples toppling in fire, spark, and smoke, the blaze devouring rows of houses. Through her tears she watched the town of her father's birth disappear in flames.

This oldest son at her side, John Quincy Adams, would become the sixth president of the United States, as her husband was to be the second. It is unlikely that any idea of these future events crossed the mind of Abigail Adams at this historic moment. But her heart held the dream that her children would live in a free land. It was important to her that they witness these unfolding events as a family committed to Liberty's cause. As the British regulars began mounting Breed's Hill, Abigail sensed that this was "perhaps the decisive day on which the fate of America depends."

· · ·

On this Saturday afternoon, June 17, 1775, thousands in the Boston area found some observation post from which to watch the coming battle. Spectators were perched on rooftop and hillcrest, on belfry and lighthouse, and even in the crow's nests of the ships in the harbor. No battle in all history had ever had such a gallery! To Abigail Adams and the thousands who stared in fearful wonder at the advancing British, the question was the same: would the rebels fight or flee?

Nothing can terrify green troops like artillery. And the British batteries now poured a deadly hail of cannon fire into the Yankee positions. Even more appalling were the oncoming regiments, each rank of three hundred men stretching the width of the battlefield, followed by another solid, compact rank, and still another. They marched to a steady drumbeat, advancing like death.

The redcoats drew closer. And still not a shot was fired from the rebel fort. Inside the redoubt, the word went up and down the line, "Hold your fire!" Each man battled his own inner terror. Knuckles were taut and white on gun barrels as the men resisted the wild urge to squeeze the trigger.

At last came the command; the Yankees fired. From the fort burst an exploding shock of doom. The redcoats reeled and dropped. It was as though a fiery wall had fallen on them. Shaken by the force of the blast, the earth seemed to fall away beneath their feet. The forward British line crumbled and the ranks behind staggered and wavered.

The slope before the fort was now an anthill. The redcoats turned and ran! Officers roared commands to keep their men in line, waved swords, and threatened with their pistols. But the British charge had been shattered.

When the haze of gunfire lifted, spectators in the distance saw red flecks on the green cloth of the hillside. Scarlet bodies lay in tangled heaps. Some of the fallen writhed like animals, groping, burrowing for safety.

At the base of Breed's Hill, General Howe, stunned and unbelieving, regrouped his forces for a second and then a third assault. Up the hill came the redcoats, stepping over dead bodies. These were men now full of violence and pent-up fury. Their bayonets would make short work of these rebel scoundrels once they overran the fort!

Behind the earthworks, the Yankees could hardly believe their own bravery. Suddenly these were men whose nerves had turned steely. Fear had fled before the wild cry of "Liberty!" Weary, parched, their eyes blackened, bodies sweaty, they lined up to face one more British assault.

But then disaster loomed. Men calling for more gunpowder learned that there was none! Over the parapet came the charging redcoats. Hand-to-hand, the rebels fought back valiantly but hopelessly inside the fort. They clubbed with their gun butts, flailed with knives against bayonets. Fighting fiercely, they retreated.

The Battle of Bunker Hill was over. In his dispatch to London, General Gage reported that "these people show a spirit and conduct against us" that "they have never displayed before." The British governor added, "The loss we have sustained is greater than we can bear."

Abigail Adams now felt herself as closely identified with the open armed struggle as any frontline fighter. In the months ahead, this woman leader of the rebel cause spurred those around her to increased resistance against the British.

"Every foot of ground which they obtain now they must fight for," she said, "and may they purchase it at a Bunker Hill price."

OVERLEAF:
The Fight on Lexington Common
by Howard Pyle
DELAWARE ART MUSEUM
WILMINGTON, DELAWARE

The Citizen Soldier

NATHAN HALE WAS still only eighteen years old when, fresh from Yale College, he proposed a "daring experiment" for the Connecticut village of New London. Although he was hired to teach the boys of the town, he would also be willing to hold a class for girls.

Where would he find the time? was the dubious query from the village elders. Nathan made a brief, earnest statement. This America would someday become a watchlight for the world, a democracy based on an educated and enlightened population of men *and women*. To further such an ideal, it would be small sacrifice to hold class before breakfast! He won a grudging consent to make the experiment.

It was still pitch dark when the handsome young schoolmaster began his long day, building a hearthfire and sweeping out his classroom. By 5:00 A.M. twenty young women were in their places, reciting Latin verb forms in a clear, sweet chorus. But although the Connecticut girls gave him the best of their smiles, Nathan thought only about one young woman, even if hopelessly. For his beloved Alice Adams had become Mrs. Ripley.

They had grown up together under one roof, Nathan and Alice, brought together by the marriage of her widowed mother and his own father, who had been left alone with ten children when his wife died.

Nathan couldn't remember how long ago he had begun to love Alice, or when he had first dreamed that she would someday be his wife.

But while he was still away at college, his own future uncertain, Alice was wedded to a well-to-do merchant of the town. It was the kind of arranged marriage that was often imposed in those days by the tyranny of parents. Nathan was shattered at this unexpected news. As he wept in grief, he knew he could never marry any other woman but his "Alicia."

Since his return to his home town of Coventry, Hale saw her distantly that winter, driving her horse and buggy to the greengrocer, skating on the millpond, christening her baby at church. His students knew the whole story of his unhappy love and understood the silent and sorrowful moods that came over him at times.

Nathan Hale was a gentle and thoughtful young man, and an athlete as well. Strong and lithe as a buck deer, he could swim a mile against the current of the Willimantic. He was a sharpshooter with a steady hand and eye. And he could jump in and out of three barrels in a row. He was almost a classical hero to the boys, modeling the ancient Greek ideal of a sound mind in a sound body.

Young Hale was a patriot, but not simply in the sense of being loyal to one's own country. His country—what was it? Not Britain, certainly— although he was indeed a subject of King George III. And America was still only a vast continent containing a scattering of colonies, with no identity as a nation. Hale was loyal instead to the set of democratic ideas that had flared in his mind during his college years and were now blazing into revolution.

Nathan heard the rumble of war only as distant thunder beyond the northern hills. By September, 1775, he was Lieutenant Hale of the Third Company, Seventh Connecticut Regiment, with the rebel army besieging Boston.

In December, he learned that the Alice whom he loved was now a widow at the age of nineteen. Nathan shared her grief at the death of her husband. But he felt some guilt, too, that the tragic event had also left him once again with a hope that Alice might become his wife.

With the spring thaw, the Continentals forced the British out of Boston. But instead of being in the thick of battle, Hale's company was in reserve, far behind the lines. Hale, now a captain, was happy to move with Washington's troops to what was likely to be a more active theater of war, New York. There they waited through the spring months of 1776 for the expected arrival of the enemy fleet, transporting an enlarged land army.

Young Captain Hale found quarters for his men in an old snuff mill, ran them through a course of battle training, and prepared them for the ordeal just ahead. Between times, he gave his mind freedom to think a soldier's thoughts of victory and peace and home. "To Alicia" was the title of an ardent poem which he wrote. "My thoughts are settled on the friend I love . . ."

. . .

Under a blackening sky, Hale's regiment stood at parade rest in the cobbled square of New York's old fish market. Behind him was arrayed his own company, watchful of the oncoming summer storm. The troops were assembled to hear words from Philadelphia. There, a body of delegates from every colony had been meeting sporadically for over two years, some of them fiercely committed to revolution, others clinging stubbornly to the hope of bringing the British to their senses.

The men of the Congress had first come together as wary strangers. Now at last they had resolved their differences to "mutually pledge to each other our lives, our fortunes, and our sacred honor." On July 4, 1776, they had approved the brief statement which declared the causes for breaking the last ties with England.

As Nathan Hale and his men waited in formation on the New York seaside, there suddenly came a prolonged roll as of rumbling drums. Out of the thunderheads above, the lightning flashed. A high, clear, nasal voice began reading the Declaration of Independence. "When in the course of human events . . ."

To Nathan Hale, the moving words and phrases came as promises to match his own long-dreamed-of hopes. They affirmed his "unalienable rights" to life, liberty, and the pursuit of happiness. These statements the young Connecticut Yankee translated into personal terms. He had just turned twenty-one. And beyond the war which was yet to be won he envisioned his own life, home, career, and family in a new society and a free land.

The words of the reader trailed off in a gust of rising wind. Captain Hale dismissed his company in a pelting rain. He walked to the seawall and stood watching the churning waters of the bay.

In the brief words he had just heard was the birth cry of a nation. The Declaration was a shout of defiance hurled across the sea at

34

England. Certainly it was heard on the island which he could see far down the narrows of New York bay, where the British were now massing an invading army greater than any they had ever sent out anywhere.

On a reconnaissance mission, the captain had taken a close look at the British buildup of troops on Staten Island from the opposite Long Island shore. General William Howe was gathering thirty-two thousand men. Included among Howe's striking force were not only England's finest regiments, but also nine thousand trained professional troops from some of Europe's most military-minded principalities. They were called Hessians, mercenaries leased by England from three impoverished German princes.

That summer Captain Hale carried out a number of daring missions that brought him to the notice of Washington's staff. Intelligence gathering, sabotage raids on enemy supply craft, tracking down Tories serving as British agents—these were tasks in which he excelled. Soon he was asked to become a member of a small special corps known as Knowlton's Rangers.

These men were assigned to scout the British outposts, carry out secret tasks, and act wherever needed as a highly mobile, hand-picked detachment directly responsible to the commander-in-chief. Hale was at last beginning to feel that he was serving some purpose in this war.

When the British struck in the muggy days of late August, they landed in force on Long Island. The defenders were quickly overpowered and overrun. The Continentals learned here to dread the massed batteries of the British fleet, the circling maneuvers of a highly trained foe, the ferocious bayonet assaults of the Hessians. The surviving rebels barely managed to retreat across the river to Manhattan under a cover of heavy fog.

Washington was now wondering why he had been persuaded to try to hold this indefensible island of New York. He was no born military commander, though he was to become in time the man the British would call "the old fox," full of trickery, deception and cunning. But now he was learning slowly, painfully, and proceeding on sheer dogged courage. He knew all too well that his entire army was in deadly peril of being split, surrounded, entrapped, destroyed, thus ending the war. Washington moved his headquarters up to the north end of Manhattan. British warships swarmed in the waters around the island. It was a maddening—and deadly—game, trying to guess where they would land.

One morning, a message from Washington asked for a single volunteer from Knowlton's Rangers, a man who would undertake a week-long mission behind the enemy lines. In this struggle between two mismatched armies, with the survival of the weeks-old American independence in the balance, the commander-in-chief desperately needed a secret agent he could trust.

It was explained to a meeting of Colonel Knowlton's men that "by the rules of war no soldier can be ordered on such a duty, so the General has asked for a Ranger to volunteer." The men were silent. They were prepared to risk their lives in combat. But spying was something else—a lonely errand in which a man denied his own identity, gave up his rights as a soldier, and risked dying a cur's death among enemies on some makeshift gallows.

Toward noon, a pale young man entered the meeting room. Nathan Hale had been caught up in an epidemic of fever that had run wild among the troops. He was still weak and unwell. But when he was told about the spy assignment, he volunteered at once.

The following morning Hale was summoned to Washington's headquarters. In his year as commander-in-chief, the general had already learned that his troops included quitters and traitors, cowards and scoundrels. But he had also seen men perform unbelievable deeds of courage. Washington, sober, quiet, kindly, shook Nathan Hale's hand, urging him to take care, assuring him of the importance of his mission. He had no taste for sending a young man to a possible rendezvous with a hangman. But the life and death of many, as well as the fate of the young republic, was at stake.

That September 16, 1776, Nathan Hale removed all traces of his military identity, said farewell to his friends, and vanished into an enemy world.

·   ·   ·

On the evening of September 21, 1776, General William Howe was in a trembling rage. His timetable had been carefully planned to rid Manhattan of rebel troops by the middle of October. It was his intention to be snugly quartered in New York City by the first snowfall.

But to the south and west he could now see the spreading flames of the burning town which had been evacuated by the rebels. Vandalism! He was certain of it. Sheer, wretched vandalism! The city had been deliberately put to the torch by rebel agents. Some of those who had been caught in the act were found to have connections with the Continental Army.

That evening Howe's headquarters was aroused by news of the capture of a man in civilian clothes charged with being an American spy. The captive had been pointed out by a trustworthy Tory from New Hampshire, who said he had seen a man who looked like his own cousin loitering about near the British camp. The cousin, said the informer, was actually an officer in the Continental Army. The suspect had been arrested, questioned and searched. No evidence was found to prove him a spy. General Howe ordered the man brought to him at once.

The general had been jarred by the firm July declaration of the colonies to become independent. How long would it take these fools to learn that they could not possibly win? He had bled them on Long Island. He had broken through their lines on Manhattan and forced them out of the town of New York. He knew he had them hopelessly trapped. When would these short-witted, numskulled, mule-headed simpletons end their folly? And now they had the gall to send a spy into his camp!

The curl of scorn on his lips, Howe looked into the pleasant blue eyes and found them honest, without guile. The young man's story was simple, seemingly sincere, and persuasive: he was an unemployed teacher looking for work. In his homespun rustic garb, his shoulder-length hair tied behind, he might ordinarily pass as such, unnoticed. Howe's penetrating gaze returned to the captive's face. He studied the eyes, vaguely troubled by the intelligence he saw there. And he was troubled as well by the superb physical condition of the young man. Was he more, much more, than the itinerant schoolmaster he claimed to be?

Howe's staff had been through the man's papers again and again without finding anything suspicious. As Howe watched, the search was repeated. The man's old leather portfolio was emptied and torn apart. It contained nothing but a Latin teacher's notes. There was a scrawled outline of Caesar's dull account of his campaign against ancient Gaul. Interspersed were sketches showing the battles that the Roman armies had fought long centuries ago.

37

OVERLEAF:
The Battle of Bunker Hill
by Howard Pyle
DELAWARE ART MUSEUM
WILMINGTON, DELAWARE

General Howe was growing impatient with the examination, when suddenly one of his aides was struck with a new view of the prisoner's Latin notes and drawings. See how closely they resembled the British positions around New York!

The general could discern it' all clearly now. There in the prisoner's "Roman" sketches were the British fortifications, the ships, the artillery, the lines of maneuver and attack, the position and movement of troops, their strength and armaments.

He was aghast. The set of notes left nothing unrevealed. This "schoolmaster" obviously had a keen mind and a rare talent for thorough observation. The notes disclosed everything about Howe's present operations and his future strategy.

The general's surge of anger now turned suddenly to slyness. The captive was clearly a man of high intelligence and capability. Too bad he had chosen to work for the rebel side, which probably gave him poor protection, little hope of advancement, and piddling rewards.

To the British commander's way of thought, if a man was a spy, he could probably be persuaded to become a double spy. And it was this proposition that he now offered his prisoner, in lieu of death.

The young man used few words in making it clear that his services were not for sale. There was nothing Britain could offer that would make him betray his own people.

Swiftly General Howe passed sentence, without hint of hearing or trial, and the spy was condemned to death the following morning. When he was asked his name and rank, the young man replied simply. He was Captain Nathan Hale of Coventry, Connecticut.

Hale spent that night under heavy guard. In the morning he was taken to an apple orchard where the fruit, still unharvested, glinted in the rising sun. It was a Sabbath day, but the church towers of the countryside were silent, their brass bells having long since been melted down for cannon.

In the distance a red glow and a mass of black smoke showed where the town of New York was still burning, a fourth of its buildings already destroyed. General Howe had no proof, but he strongly suspected that this spy, Nathan Hale, had organized the burning of New York just as efficiently as he had scouted the British army.

A group of British staff officers had gathered for the hanging. They wagered on two possibilities. Either Hale would finally agree to become a British spy, or else he would make a last desperate plea, groveling, begging like a coward for his young life.

After a hushed instant, the condemned man spoke in clear, quiet tones. The assembled British were thunderstruck at what they heard. "I only regret that I have but one life to lose for my country."

Then with calmness and great dignity, Nathan Hale mounted the gallows steps.

Maker of Heroes

THE HARDEST LESSON for young Thomas Paine was to learn his place.

In his native town of Thetford, England, there were the poor and lowly, the sons who meekly followed the trades of their fathers, the dutiful and pious who muttered God and king in the same breath. Paine was born to such a life. He just wasn't supposed to become a shaker of empires, a writer of moving prose, a maker of heroes.

And yet, it was Thomas Paine who dared to cry out in America the fearsome word *Independence!* at a time when most Americans still considered themselves British subjects. Later, in the darkest moment of the nation's precarious infancy he breathed glowing life into the last tiny spark of hope.

How did this penniless British tradesman happen to appear so fatefully on the scene of America's birth?

Paine had come to the capital of revolutionary America in 1775 as an ordinary man with modest ambitions. But a genuine revolution is not merely an armed struggle; it is an intellectual explosion that may burst the dam holding the pent-up creativeness in people. In Thomas Paine a concealed talent was set free.

He had never published a word in England. Here he became an editor of a Philadelphia journal and wrote brilliantly, not only on politics but on a variety of matters of social concern. He voiced enlightened views on marriage and divorce, slavery, and the rights of women to a place in public life. He discussed the danger of giving too much power not only to kings but to future presidents as well.

In the Philadelphia taverns he debated with American leaders who were still reluctant to make a clean break with the British monarchy. He realized that the delegates to the Continental Congress were trying to speak for a populace that was still largely loyal to the crown.

Paine wrote a pamphlet titled *Common Sense* which appeared in print on January 10, 1776. By mere chance, the Philadelphia newspapers on that same day carried the report of the speech of King George III to the opening session of Parliament. In the royal message the monarch refused to discuss any of the grievances of the colonies. Instead, the king ordered the Americans to give up their rebelliousness. He was anxious, he said, to prevent bloodshed, but added that he had increased the size of his land and sea forces in order to "put a speedy end to these disorders."

"When the unhappy and deluded multitude, against whom this force will be directed, shall become sensible of their error," stated King George, "I shall be ready to receive the misled with tenderness and mercy."

Unwittingly, the king in his arrogance had opened the minds and hearts of Americans to Thomas Paine's *Common Sense*.

. . .

"O ye that love mankind! Ye that dare oppose not only the tyranny but the tyrant, stand forth!"

Paine's words were pure fire, and they burned their way into the consciousness of a scattered populace not yet sure they were ready for nationhood. Until this moment, separation from England was a question most Americans had not cared to face. But Paine cried out, " 'Tis time to part!" And he explained with clarity and eloquence why these colonies must now find their own way in the world. On each of his fifty pages the reasons were set out with human understanding and persuasive force.

"We have it in our power to begin the world over," Paine called out to the far reaches of these separate colonies. "Let each of us hold out to his neighbor the hearty hand of fellowship..." The pamphlet, signed simply by "an unknown Englishman," convinced by its logic and its facts.

Common Sense became common reading, as were the Scriptures. Its simple language was read aloud at village crossroads and by children in schools, in the front lines of battlefields and from the pulpits of country churches. Ten thousand copies were sold, and then a hundred thousand. The printing presses in every colony were thumping them out as the demand grew. And soon they were being sold as widely in Germany and France as in America.

Washington, who had earlier shunned the very notion of separation from Britain, now wrote to a friend, "My countrymen will come reluctantly to the idea of independence, but time and persecution bring wonderful things to pass; and by the letters I have lately received from Virginia, I find *Common Sense* working a powerful change in the minds of men."

Six months later, when the Declaration of Independence was announced, the American people were prepared for it. Paine had set them thinking about defending their own land and governing it in their own way.

That summer of 1776 Paine joined the Continental Army, which was quartered in New York. He was almost forty years old, of middle height, with a wiry body well-built to withstand hardship and hard work. Although he was now well known as the author of *Common Sense*, Paine lived as a common soldier among his comrades-in-arms. But unlike his companions, he sometimes visited with the commander-in-chief. Washington was a man without close friends, aloof and alone. But he took to this swarthy, intense Englishman. Washington shared with him his dire problems at this critical time of the war.

By the late summer of 1776, the rebels had been driven from New York. The Continental Army was now reduced to a few thousand men, half-starved, half-armed, half-clothed. Across New Jersey they fled from the pursuing enemy, which often appeared behind them within musket range. Crossing the rivers, they barely saved themselves by destroying the bridges behind them. In the dreary remains of the year, rebel defeats followed one upon another with disheartening regularity.

The men saw Paine writing by the campfire late at night and knew he was sending reports to the newspapers on the war's progress. It was "a period of distresses" which Paine tried to describe truthfully in his dispatches without adding to the gloom which now clouded the rebel cause.

For ninety miles, from Fort Lee in New Jersey to the Pennsylvania border, the wretched troops marched through slashing rains and ice storms. Many were barefoot as they plodded along the jagged, frozen, washed-out roads. The artillery horses were up to their bellies in mud,

and the supply wagons were hopelessly mired. The men lifted heavy clods of clay with every step. Half-crazed with hunger and cold, they occasionally had enough spirit to sing a feeble marching song, "Yankee Doodle," which acquired a good many new verses, the lines often ending with "retreat" and "defeat."

This was an army on its last legs. Discouraged and weary, they reached the broad Delaware River in December, 1776. Washington's men rounded up all the boats they could use for the crossing in the vicinity of Trenton, destroyed the rest, and crossed the river to the Pennsylvania side. Just behind them, the pursuing Hessian troops occupied Trenton.

Thomas Paine knew fully how desperate was the rebel cause, how close was the American Revolution to its last dying gasp. He had a strong faith in himself and in the power of his writing, but he wondered what mere words could do in this hopeless situation. And yet he had so much

Washington Reviewing His Troops
by William Trego
VALLEY FORGE HISTORICAL SOCIETY

to say to this country and to his fellow soldiers who seemed part of a forlorn cause.

In the rebel camp one wintry night, Paine began writing in a fit of passion, burning energy at a white heat. In the late hours of darkness he put together his ideas, feelings, and hopes, the candlelight reflecting in his triangular face, in his dark, deep-socketed eyes. Exhausted, he finally drew a blanket around him, dropped to the cold, drenched ground, and fell into a deep sleep.

Early the next morning, he was on his way to Philadelphia to find a printer. The capital city of the Revolution was in panic, aware of the enemy only twenty-five miles away. The people, Paine found, were in "a deplorable and melancholy condition, afraid to speak and almost to think, the public presses stopped, and nothing in circulation but fears and falsehoods."

As for Washington, camped on the Delaware, he was spending these troubled days and nights mulling his chances of carrying on the war once his soldiers had completed these remaining days of their enlistment.

"Your imagination can scarce extend to a situation more distressing than mine," he wrote to a kinsman. "Our only dependence now is upon the speedy enlistment of a new army. If this fails, the game will be pretty well up."

.   .   .

In the gray morning of December 19, 1776, the post rider from Philadelphia brought General George Washington a printed sheet of paper. It was an ink-smudged first copy of Thomas Paine's *The Crisis*. In his headquarters on the Delaware River bluff, the commander might have been hoping for a detachment of fresh troops, a load of warm clothes for his men, or another month of days in this dwindling year. But as Washington read the little broadside in his hand, he knew that here he had something of equal worth. Paine's words were a tonic. After he read *The Crisis* a second time, a glow filled his tired body. He was stirred with the feeling of new hope and set to work on a plan.

The general had almost given up trying to persuade his soldiers to reenlist or even to stay on another month. His officers were disheartened. And now Washington proposed to his staff that this ghost of a rebel army take the offensive against the British! His men looked at him as though he had gone mad. Nevertheless, the pitiful little force on the river bank prepared to attack.

In these last days of December, the weather had turned wild. The storm of one day was exceeded by the gale-powered fury of the next. And the rebels had little shelter. Far across the river in Trenton, they could see the lights of the Hessian garrison through the sleet.

The Continentals were men without morale, dull-eyed and numb with cold. They had let their whiskers grow, and they no longer tried to cope with their dirt and raggedness. Many were covered with a scabby itch for which there was no known remedy. The quality of their rations was poor. Occasionally, to vary the monotony, they clubbed a squirrel and roasted it over a fire on the end of a ramrod.

Their term of enlistment was over at year's end. If they could somehow stay alive for these few remaining days, it was home sweet home. As for the war and the Continental Army—well, they shrugged, maybe it was all over for the Americans anyway. Or let others take a turn and serve as they had.

Washington, who often appeared to his men as a stern martinet, was filled with sympathy for them. "The soldiers eat every kind of horse food but hay," he reported to Congress. "The fortitude—the long and great suffering of this army—is unexampled in history."

On Christmas day, sleet came raging out of a pewter sky. The rebel soldiers could hardly believe that Washington was going ahead with his scheme of attack. But here they were, loading up for the river crossing.

By nightfall, the sleet changed to cold rain. The loading of boats had become painfully slow, the men inching their way up and down the slippery embankment. The high wind howled through the woods. Heavy slabs of ice, churned by the surging waters of the river, would make the crossing risky. Boats loaded with horses and artillery rocked ominously at the water's edge. The men knew that through the next twenty-four hours there would not be an instant in which they would be warm or dry. Perhaps they would drown in the swirling waters of the ice-choked river, or die with a long Hessian bayonet in the chest.

Washington chose this moment for a pause. Up and down the river bank the soldiers huddled in small groups around shielded lamps. Paine's *The Crisis* was being read aloud.

The opening words brought gasps and a few sobs. "These are the times that try men's souls," it began. "The summer soldier and the sunshine patriot will, in this crisis, shrink from the service of their country; but he that stands it *now* deserves the loving thanks of man and woman."

49

OVERLEAF:
Washington Crossing the Delaware
by Emanuel Leutze
THE METROPOLITAN MUSEUM OF ART
GIFT OF JOHN S. KENNEDY, 1897

The men listened in silence. Every word that Paine had written seemed to speak to their wretched condition, to the despair that gripped them.

"I thank God that I fear not," wrote this Englishman who had become an American patriot. "I see no real cause for fear.

"By perseverance and fortitude, we have the prospect of a glorious issue; by cowardice and submission, the sad choice of a variety of evils—a ravaged country, habitations without safety, and slavery without hope."

In the early morning hours, the Americans crossed the Delaware and struck the enemy. The rebels took the enemy garrison completely by surprise. After only a few fierce but scattered skirmishes the white flag of surrender appeared.

Not a single American died in the battle. The Hessians suffered a large number of casualties. Washington took nine hundred prisoners, as well as munitions, blankets, food, medicine, clothes. The tiny rebel army was exhausted but jubilant.

In the east, General Cornwallis, British commander of the entire Jersey front, had news of Washington's exploits. So the rebel leader wanted to play the fox, did he? Well, Cornwallis had chased and cornered and bagged many a fox. And now the hunt was on.

Moving swiftly in force, he reached Trenton and took over half the town. The trap which Cornwallis had devised was to pin Washington between Trenton's mill pond and the raging Delaware River. Cornwallis went to bed that night planning to make his kill in the morning. Across the pond, all was silence behind the line of Washington's campfires.

Just about dawn, British sentries heard thunder from the northeast. Or was it cannon fire? By the light of day, Cornwallis put a glass to his eye and studied the rebel positions across the pond. But there was nothing and no one to be seen! Washington had slipped away in the night. His rebel army had silently circled Cornwallis's camp, sped to Princeton, and attacked the redcoats there. After an American artillery barrage and a bayonet charge, the British surrendered the Princeton garrison!

Trenton and Princeton were not great battles in size, but these victories came at a moment which swelled their importance. The young nation and its citizen army took heart from these triumphs. In one of the war's darkest moments, Washington had won the chance of rebuilding his army and winning public support.

Across this land, Paine had become the voice of hope and reason. A series of *Crisis* papers followed the first, building the confidence of the people in their own strength and in the justice of their cause. Americans fought "not to enslave, but to set a country free," Paine said, "and to make room upon the earth for honest men to live in."

The Rifleman

EVEN BEFORE THE first shot of the Revolution, Daniel Morgan was well decorated with battle scars. He was a Virginia frontiersman. During the French and Indian wars of the 1750s, young Daniel served the British as a wagoner, freighting heavy cargoes of military supplies over rugged mountains and across a vast wilderness.

After a tavern brawl, during which he struck an officer, Daniel was court-martialed by the British and sentenced to five hundred lashes of the whip. Strapping guardsmen took turns flaying the young wagoner, ripping his back mercilessly in a vain effort to make Morgan beg for mercy. But the harder they pounded, the more the American held his rage inside himself. Morgan lived through the ordeal out of sheer stubborn will to survive. That brutal flogging became a memory engraved in his flesh, a bitter grievance to be settled with Britain.

Morgan was a big man in every dimension, burly, powerful, vigorous. In appearance, he was long limbed, with a massive trunk and a face that seemed hewn from a solid walnut block. Between wars, the Virginian was a frontier farmer who cleared his land of stumps and rocks by his own muscle power. He never learned how to spell, scorned fancy uniforms, and preferred the company of backwoodsmen like himself. Dan Morgan was a natural leader of men.

Early in 1777, Morgan, now a colonel in the Continental army, began forming a corps of fighters who had a distinct preference for a rather unusual weapon. From boyhood, these men had learned to use the rifle instead of the more commonly known musket. The youngster who went hunting in the Virginia backwoods was expected to bring back a squirrel for every bullet in his pouch, a squirrel neatly shot through the head. A lifetime of training had made Morgan and his neighbors crack shots with the rifle.

This weapon was being handmade by frontier gunsmiths of German and Swiss origins. In contrast to the smoothbore musket, the rifle had a long barrel with spiral grooves inside. It hurled out a tightly-fitted bullet with tremendous force into spinning flight, and it had a remarkably long range.

This long, slender rifle had not been used in any previous war. In combat, the weapon had serious shortcomings. It required extra time and skill for loading. It was not fitted with a bayonet. But its effective range was twice that of the musket, and in the hands of an expert, it was an accurate and awesome weapon.

General George Washington had seen what the rifle could do. Now, in the spring of 1777, he was writing to his fellow Virginian, Colonel Daniel Morgan, urging that he bring his riflemen into action against a new threat to the rebel cause that had suddenly appeared in the far north.

In Canada, Britain's General John Burgoyne was putting together a second army of vast size and striking power. Burgoyne was the author of what became known as the "Grand Strategy," a plan for dividing and conquering America by a single, unified masterstroke. The plan was to swing a bisecting line of control down through the heart of the colonies, from Montreal to New York, thus linking one British center of strength to the other.

For the success of his scheme, Burgoyne counted on General Howe to plunge upward from the southern end of the Hudson to join him. But Burgoyne pondered too whether he could carry out the master plan alone, if necessary. He was a tall, imposing commander with a strong jaw and flashing eyes. His nickname was "Gentleman Johnny." He was a peacock, a talented, strutting performer. His stage—before he landed on American shores—had been the House of Commons, the battlefield, and the theater itself for which he had written several successful plays. He was addicted to card playing and horse racing.

The British general was a gambler at heart, and in his Grand Strategy the stakes were high. But of all the possible risks, Gentleman Johnny could hardly have foreseen an "old wagoner" and his frontier friends.

·   ·   ·

In a piney wood near Fredericksburg, Virginia, a red apple went sailing through the morning air. A shot rang out. When a group of men examined the apple, they found that the center of it had been neatly cored by a bullet. Colonel Daniel Morgan warmly shook the hand of the young rifleman who had fired the shot, and informed him that he was now a qualified member of "Morgan's Rangers."

For weeks the colonel had been selectively recruiting men for his rifle corps. Through the bright days of June, 1777, the riflemen, with Morgan at their head, marched northward, hand-picking new recruits as they went. The colonel was accepting only trained marksmen, sharp-eyed and cool-nerved.

Morgan's Rangers were a lanky, towering group, each man carrying more than five feet of rifle tucked comfortably in the crook of his arm. They enjoyed showing off their shooting skill, and at every chance they staged contests among themselves. They were dressed frontier style, these riflemen, in fringed buckskin leggins and moccasins, a buck's tail stuck in their hats. A fellow Virginian, Patrick Henry, had given them their battle slogan. The patriot's words in the Virginia House of Burgesses were emblazoned across their chests: "Liberty or Death!"

The "old wagoner," as Morgan called himself, was no stickler for strict discipline and military decorum. His men were devoted to him because he was one of them, showed real concern for their safety, and saw to it that they were as comfortable, clean, well fed, and healthy as possible.

To his Virginia corps, the colonel added frontiersmen from other colonies. Morgan's Rangers developed a high morale and traded their lore among themselves. The Virginians showed how they corrected rifle sightings for the effect of the wind on the course of the bullet's long flight. The Pennsylvanians displayed their method of wrapping the bullet in a tiny buckskin patch soaked in bear grease. This made it easier to ram the lead slug down into the barrel. And the bore was much cleaner after firing.

The Yankee highlanders shared with the other riflemen their cocky marching song, which went like this:

Why come ye hither, redcoats,
Across the briny water?
Why come ye hither, redcoats,
Like bullocks to the slaughter?
Oh listen to the singing
Of the trumpet wild and free!
Full soon you'll hear the barking
Of the rifle from the tree!

Gathering of the Mountain Men
by Lloyd Branson
TENNESSEE STATE MUSEUM

That summer of 1777 Burgoyne was moving steadily down the invasion route from Canada with ten thousand men, one of the best-equipped British armies ever to take to the field. He carried with him powerful artillery, a supporting column of German mercenaries, a large corps of Indian scouts, and some of the ablest of the British field commanders. Fort Ticonderoga fell readily to their assault, and it seemed that nothing could halt their progress down the river valley. However, Howe's army from the south had not yet begun to move toward the juncture with Burgoyne.

Privately, General Howe had decided not to fit himself into Burgoyne's Grand Strategy. He had his own scheme for glory that involved moving not northward, but southward toward capture of the rebel capital of Philadelphia. The two generals, deeply involved in London politics, continued throughout the war to pursue their own personal strategies and ambitions.

Meanwhile, Washington sent a force to block Burgoyne's advance. This was a hastily assembled army under General Horatio Gates, including Morgan's Rangers. To Daniel Morgan, Washington penned a note explaining why he was sending the riflemen into action against Burgoyne's army. "I know of no corps so likely to check their progress," he wrote.

That was high confidence in a tiny force of men armed only with a strange and untested combat weapon. Morgan arrived on the upper Hudson with 331 able-bodied riflemen for what history would know as the Battle of Saratoga.

. . .

On the morning of September 19, 1777, a soft fog filtered up from the Hudson River to cover the gentle hills and settle into the ravines. Burgoyne's army was moving southward, uncertain of when and how they would meet resistance.

North of Albany, British scouts came back with reports of enemy activity just ahead. Burgoyne fortified himself behind a riverside farmstead. The owner, a man named Freeman, had long since abandoned the place, leaving only an old dog and some unharvested grain.

Beyond a patch of cleared acres surrounded by thick woods was the American force, made up mainly of half-trained, poorly armed men. A few had seen combat, some came out of local militias, but most were green, untried recruits. There was only one bayonet for every three muskets among them and not half enough of what an army needs in order to win.

On the hill behind the rebels, two high-ranking American officers were locked in a bitter quarrel. General Horatio Gates, a former British army officer, was a pettifogging paperwork general, more comfortable with his maps and reports than among his troops.

Gates's decisions were being vigorously disputed by his associate, General Benedict Arnold, a proud, impetuous man of fierce temper and strong will. Arnold seemed to need constant acclaim, and he never felt that he was being adequately recognized or rewarded. He had a reputation as a headstrong field commander, leading the charges with the cry, "Follow me!"

Colonel Morgan found himself in the middle between these two snarling, bickering commanders. He had a good mind to knock their heads together. Instead, he went down to deploy his men for what was to become an afternoon of ferocious battle.

The British attacked in three columns. Laying down a heavy artillery barrage, the redcoats moved steadily across the fields of Freeman's Farm. Burgoyne's four crack regiments came through the center, sweeping through the clearing. But as the advance force of three hundred men approached the woods, Morgan's rifles went into action. Every British officer but one went down with a bullet wound. And the riflemen proceeded to pick off the redcoats as fast as they could fire.

Flushed with success, the riflemen came out of the woods, yelling and charging into the clearing. Wildly, they headed toward disaster. Morgan was in panic. "I am ruined," he cried out. "My men are scattered God knows where!"

Many had plunged toward the British bayonets, forgetting their rifles were useless in hand-to-hand combat. Morgan blew frantically on his homemade hunting whistle, which he used to assemble and command his men. The sound of his turkey call brought the riflemen back to safety. They had momentarily lost their heads, but they would not make this mistake again.

The fighting raged into the late afternoon. Possession of the open ground passed back and forth. But steadily from the woods came the deadly fire of the riflemen. Morgan's firepower was not like the volley of muskets. His men were ordered to fire singly and at will. The gobble of his turkey call kept them moving to the best advantage. Climbing the trees, the riflemen picked their targets carefully, making every shot count.

Both sides could easily have claimed the day's victory—and they did. Burgoyne lost a third of his force. The Americans had heavy casualties as well. Damaged, weakened, exhausted, the rival armies backed off.

During the next two weeks, there was no rest for the riflemen. They roamed stealthily through the woods, sniping at the British from behind cover. The redcoats never quite got used to this American weapon. Again and again they made the mistake of forgetting its range and its deadly accuracy.

Day and night, the marksmanship of Morgan's men took its toll. For the redcoats, the safety of distance had vanished. The rifleman squeezed the trigger when he saw red in his sights, and another British soldier was dead. Perched like a nighthawk in a high treetop, the sharpshooter fired at a glow of candlelight, the glint of a brass button, the sound of a footfall, a moving shadow.

On October 7, an aide reported to General Gates that the British were again moving into battle positions. "Order Morgan to begin the game!" the general snapped.

The foliage had turned wine colored and golden on the soft hills. But around the little farm, the day built quickly to a fury of belching fire and deafening sound. The battle advantage rolled back and forth. Each side drove in savagely, only to be turned back. The artillery fired fast at point-blank range. More than once, a big cannon, griddle-hot, changed hands. Turned around, the gun was fired at those who had just manned it.

Throughout the battle, the deadly fire of the snipers continued with uncanny accuracy. The redcoats glanced at the dark woods in terror. There the riflemen squinted through their sights, spotting their targets one at a time. Through the soft-ploughed earth the British rolled their six-pounders, the men straining at the wheel spokes. Morgan's men singled out the gunners and one by one the cannons were silenced.

Morgan had coached his men to recognize the British uniforms and the insignia of rank. The game they played that day was to pick the highest-ranking officers as targets. "Aim for the epaulets!" they shouted to one another.

Through the smoke of battle, the rebels could see one British officer who seemed to inject his own high courage into his faltering troops. Mounted on a superb gray charger, General Simon Fraser flashed in brilliant color along the thinning redcoat line, rallying the men for still another assault. At a signal from Morgan, one of the riflemen shinnied up a tall maple and put his cheek to his gunstock. The crack of a single gun echoed in the high trees. The rifle bullet, whirling in flight, found its intended mark. General Fraser, mortally wounded, slumped in his saddle and fell to the ground.

The advancing British line halted and then fell away. From that moment, their power seemed spent. Pinned against the Hudson, Burgoyne no longer had any choices, not even retreat. On a crisp October morning, ten days later, he surrendered to the rebels the remains of a British army. In the Battle of Saratoga, the Americans had won their greatest victory of the war.

When news of Saratoga reached Europe, the reaction was strong and swift. France, still weighing America's chances of victory, now threw its strength to the rebel side. Within weeks the French government recognized the struggling new nation. This, in time, would be followed by aid in land troops, ships, and supplies.

The British commander took his defeat in a gentlemanly manner. He had gambled and lost. Burgoyne sought out the rifle corps leader. He shook Morgan's hand, saying, "Sir, you command the finest regiment in the world." Burgoyne later admitted that half of his losses were men hit by rifle bullets.

Strangely, it was not Morgan but two other men who took for themselves all the glory of the Saratoga victory. Before the war's end, one of them, General Horatio Gates, would turn out to be a jealous plotter against Washington. The other, General Benedict Arnold, would soon become a traitor in the pay of the British.

Daniel Morgan did not linger long at the ceremonies of the American victory and the British surrender. With his buckskin garb and homespun manners he was not at home in the brilliant spectacle of a dress parade. The "old wagoner" packed his rifle, turkey whistle, hunting shirt, and all. Morgan was ready for his next orders.

A Man Named Jones

A SMALL MAN in seafarer's garb arrived in Philadelphia in July, 1775, and offered his services in the American navy.

At the moment there was no such navy—he knew that. But he would be willing to organize and run it, said the stranger in a thick Scottish burr. His name, he declared, was John Paul Jones. Still in his twenties, he had been for many years a British shipmaster in the West Indies trade.

It turned out that the stranger was a man of mystery. There was some doubt that his name was Jones at all. It was rumored that he had stabbed a mutinous deckhand to death on one of his ships, and that another had died after being severely flogged. The gossip was that Jones had captained ships in the slave traffic. Supposedly, he had also operated for a time as a pirate!

There is no record that the Continental Congress ever investigated the truth about Jones's shadowy background. But by December, 1775, John Paul Jones was a first lieutenant aboard the first ships flying American colors. In an effort to confront British sea power, the Congress had put together a makeshift armada. Made up of a score of assorted craft, there was not a genuine warship among them. Most were freighters, passenger ships, whalers, or merchantmen on which a few guns had been mounted. In this little fleet, Jones soon became a captain.

Captain Jones raised at his masthead a strange striped banner which pictured a rattlesnake and the defiant slogan, "Don't Tread on Me!" During the next two years, he ranged up and down the American coast, carrying out his orders to "distress the enemy by all means in your power." A raging wave of destruction, he ran ferociously at ships flying the Union Jack from Newfoundland to the West Indies. Scores of British transport and supply ships were captured or sunk by this sea raider who managed to stay well out of the gun range of the mighty British men-o'-war. Again and again, he returned to his home port with a small fleet of captured prizes in his wake.

His crew admired their captain's seamanship and fighting courage, but they had little affection for him. Though he had long since flung away his cat-o'-nine-tails, the seamen feared his temper and avoided him as though he were a seagoing rattlesnake. Jones was never able to shake off his old reputation as a cruel despot. Aboard ship, he kept to himself, a peevish man, still fairly young, but full of old hatreds and dark moods. In battle, he was a demon who never gave up, and he often won by his sheer stubborn will to win.

The captain was never seen except in neat and proper uniform. He was a small-scale man, well proportioned, with angular shoulders, delicate wrists and ankles. His face was bony, his black hair drawn into a tight queue.

Proud and ambitious, he carried on a running dispute with his superiors. From its earliest days, the American navy was waterlogged with petty politics, favoritism, naval dogma, and seniority lists. In his efforts to secure larger commands and bigger ships, Jones was constantly frustrated. He had strong opinions and he used little tact in expressing them. The captain was certain that he knew better than anyone else how the navy should be run. And he refused to salute his way up the ladder of rank. In short, he had a talent for making enemies in high places.

Nevertheless, by the end of October, 1777, Jones had command of a newly built, one-hundred-foot war sloop, the *Ranger*, and orders that would carry him to another part of the world. At Portsmouth, New Hampshire, he slipped his moorings, and favorable winds wafted him onto the high seas.

The *Ranger* was a snug, trim vessel, and Jones now shook out every shred of sail he could hoist to test her speed. He was bound for Europe, his destination the busy English coast with its many harbors and seaports.

This was the mercantile center of the nation that ruled the waves.

In the weeks ahead, the *Ranger* became a masked marauder, not openly identified as an American vessel or a ship of war. Within sight of the shore, Jones pillaged up and down the British coast. Scores of richly laden craft became his prizes. Burning, scuttling, riddling, capturing British shipping, the captain brought the war home to England.

In April of 1778, John Paul Jones faced the Scottish coast for a strange kind of homecoming. He was full of wrath over British outrages in his adopted land. And he was bitterly resentful that captured American seamen were rotting in British jails and prison ships, with no chance of exchange or release.

In the captain's mind had grown a brazen scheme. It was not merely vengeance that he sought. Jones held the notion that England would relent in its treatment of Americans if the imperial nation could be made to feel some counterblow on its own shores.

And where was this bold captain better able to deliver such a blow than on that part of the British Isles that he knew best? These were the thoughts of John Paul Jones as his sails moved him, silent as the moonlight, toward the seaport of Whitehaven. This was the port he had left as a seaman apprentice at the age of twelve, almost twenty years before.

In the darkness, the *Ranger* entered the harbor. With a band of his crewmen, Jones went ashore before dawn. First, they entered the seaside fortress of the town, scaling the wall by climbing on each other's shoulders. They tied up the sleeping sentries. Swiftly they spiked the fort's gun batteries, making certain that no cannon fire would interfere with their escape. Next, Jones led his men down to the harbor. With torches they set fire to the merchant ships moored there. Meeting hardly any resistance and with no one injured, Jones fled as rapidly as he had arrived.

It was dawn now as the *Ranger* took flight, and the astonished townsfolk were crowded at the water's edge. There were many who remembered the boy who had once lived hereabouts. They had never thought he would turn out to be such a rogue, pirate, villain!

Before the *Ranger* turned homeward, Jones performed a few more exploits. One misfired—a daring plan to kidnap a British lord, who was not home when the American raiders came to call.

One day, off the Scottish coast, Jones spied an enemy sail which turned out to be the British war sloop, the *Drake*. She was well manned and well armed. Jones made for her, and a brief, furious battle followed.

The American commander showed extraordinary skill in seamanship and firing tactics. Swiftly he turned his guns on the *Drake*'s sailing and steering gear, putting her quickly at his mercy. He could have sent her to the bottom, but suddenly he was struck with a bright notion. What would the world say if John Paul Jones seized a superior British warship on England's coast and took her captive to France? The idea was too good to resist, and he soon had the *Drake* in tow. A few days later he brought his prize triumphantly to Brest.

With his raids, Jones set London on its ear. He had made fools of the naval ministry, having destroyed an enormous quantity of shipping. As for his land raids on the English coast, no one had dared to do that for a hundred years!

The government dispatched orders that Jones was wanted, dead or alive. The Admiralty sent out its fastest and most powerful warships to catch him. But the spunky American captain could not be caught.

No longer satisfied with the sloop *Ranger*, Captain Jones was now imbued with the hope of securing a more powerful warship, with himself at the head of a raiding squadron. However, if Jones had been impatient with the delays that hampered him in America, he found himself caught in an even stickier web of politics and intrigue in France. He turned to the man who had become his good friend, the wise and genial American envoy, Benjamin Franklin.

But even with Franklin's help, endless obstacles kept Jones land bound while he was making arrangements with the French government, which promised to help him secure a new command. He was soon running out of time and patience. The flagship which he finally accepted was a sixty-year-old hulk that had spent years in the China trade long after she was declared unseaworthy.

In renaming his vessel, Jones paid a tribute to his friend, Franklin, whose book *Poor Richard's Almanac* was being widely read in France under the title *Les Maximes du Bonhomme Richard*. Jones named his ship the *Bonhomme Richard*. Forty guns were mounted on her, an assortment picked up from the naval scrap piles of France. On a test cruise, Jones soon discovered the *Richard* was leaky, slow, clumsy, rotted out.

The captain did the best he could in gathering up seamen. He finally signed on a motley crew on which he could place little reliance. He was told that seven ships had been assigned to his command. But he was given no assurance that they would respond to his orders.

If any observers viewed Jones's outbound flotilla as a unified fighting force, they couldn't have been farther from the truth. Ill feeling simmered on every vessel. Among the messmates of Jones's flagship there was little loyalty to the captain. A large part of the sullen crew were captured English seamen who were likely to jump ship, mutiny, or aid the enemy at any opportune time. As for the rest of the fleet, each shipmaster and officer was looking out for his own safety, profit, and glory in this venture. Once at sea, they ignored the fleet commander's orders. The treacherous master of the *Alliance*, Captain Landais, bitterly hated Jones and would betray him in a critical moment of battle.

· · ·

Undaunted, John Paul Jones now set a course toward his boldest ventures. From France, the bows of Jones's little squadron plowed the seas northward. They took British prizes as they went, filling their holds with prisoners and either seizing or sinking enemy ships.

On the morning of September 23, 1779, Jones spied a flock of white sails that made his heart leap. This was a forty-one-ship British convoy in the Baltic trade. By dusk, he was within hailing distance of the convoy's escorts. These were two mighty British ships of war—the *Serapis* of fifty guns, and the *Countess of Scarborough*, mounting twenty-two. They were floating fortresses, carrying tier upon tier of wide-throated guns, loaded and primed, small flaming torches at each cannon ready to touch off thunder.

"What ship is that?" came the trumpeted query from the *Serapis*. This was a formal little game, stalling for time while the gun crews worked through a train of operations that readied them for the command to fire.

"Come a little nearer and I will tell you," Jones replied, playing the game.

"What are you laden with?" came from the Englishman, now abreast and at close range.

"With round, grape-, and double-headed shot!" was the defiant reply.

At almost the same instant, the warships exchanged broadsides. In the first fire, three of the *Richard's* biggest guns burst. Captain Jones ordered that the remaining eighteen-pounders be abandoned. The *Serapis*, with a crushing superiority of heavy weapons, now raked the American ship fore and aft. Her eighteen-pound shot smashed holes through both sides of the *Richard*.

The agony of the long battle had begun. Circling each other, the two ships maneuvered to inflict the most damage and take the least. The *Serapis* quickly showed herself to be faster and more maneuverable than the *Richard*.

One whole tier of the *Richard's* guns had now been silenced. The British ship unloosed rapid and destructive fire from its two gun decks, its eighteen-pounders splintering the hull of Jones's flagship. As the battle became intense, Jones's fleet vanished beyond the horizon. The British *Countess of Scarborough*, not yet engaged by any of Jones's consorts, fired broadsides into the stern of the *Richard*.

The opposing captains were now clearly aware of the British superiority in the battle. The *Serapis* had proved herself a sturdier and faster ship, manned by a larger and better-trained crew, with more and heavier guns. At this point, the British Captain Pearson demanded to know whether Jones was ready to strike his colors and surrender. Then came John Paul Jones's deathless reply:

"I have not yet begun to fight!"

Outgunned, the American commander knew that his only hope lay in closing the distance between the two ships. He managed to ram his vessel broadside into the Britisher. The crash loosed the *Serapis's* forestays. Jones himself bound the lines firmly to the foremast of his ship.

"We've got her now," the American skipper shouted. "Throw on the grappling irons and stand by for boarding!" The two ships were now bound fast, cannons muzzle-to-muzzle. Each deck was strewn with the dead and wounded. Fire spread from the forecastle of the *Serapis* to its rigging and then to the ropework of the *Bonhomme Richard*.

Jones sent his men aloft with muskets. Small arms would have to answer for the big cannons he didn't have. From the high rigging, the *Richard's* men raked the decks of the *Serapis* with gunfire. Eleven men in succession were shot down at the helm.

One of the *Richard's* seamen crawled far out on a lofty yardarm and tossed a smoldering hand grenade to the deck of the enemy vessel. The grenade bounced about, then dropped between decks, bursting in a pile of loose gunpowder. The explosion set the two interlocked ships rocking furiously. Burning debris showered into the night sky. A score of British seamen were killed in the blast and a set of starboard cannons were demolished.

At this moment, the *Alliance* appeared. Glimpsing the American colors, Jones had a brief moment of joy. But to the commander's horror, the guns of the oncoming *Alliance* opened up against the *Bonhomme Richard!* It seemed that Landais had gone completely mad.

The crewmen and officers of the *Richard* shouted to the *Alliance* captain that he was bombarding the wrong ship. "Stop, or you'll sink us!" they pleaded. But the hate-crazed Landais continued to pour cannonballs into the disabled *Richard*.

Jones's ship was now ablaze, the dry old timbers crackling and the flames licking at the tar-and-pitch caulking. Below decks, the *Richard* was filling with water, the sea flooding in through its gaping wounds. But the foundering American ship was still attached to the *Serapis* in a death grip. Jones refused to give up.

The battle by moonlight had been going on for three hours. On the lower decks of *Serapis*, its remaining guns were still blazing away. Jones now had nothing but three nine-pounders, one of which he manned himself. He directed grapeshot at the mainmast of *Serapis*. Finally, the riddled mast toppled, falling overboard.

The *Richard* was settling deeper in the water. Jones released his prisoners from the brig and put them to work at the pumps. Flames from the blazing deck reached upward, catching the shredded sails, spars, and cordage. Waterlogged, the hull was agape with huge holes. The rudder hung loose and useless. The flagship's fragmented decking was ready to collapse into the hold. And still Jones fought on, demanding to know whether the British captain was ready to quit!

It was close to midnight when Captain Richard Pearson at last struck his colors. He surrendered his sword to John Paul Jones. Suddenly silence settled over the moonlit sea.

The *Bonhomme Richard* was cut adrift. The ship did not stay afloat very long. Sinking slowly, it was a coffin for more than half of its crew, killed in the fight.

Patched up, the crippled *Serapis* made sail for the coast of Holland. Two weeks later, a crowd of Dutchmen lined the docks at Dunkirk to see the strangest of sights. The *Serapis* slowly made its way into the harbor. It was a hag ship, a battered and burnt ruin, its hull pocked with openings, canvas tattered, decks strewn with wreckage. At the rails swarmed seven hundred battle-weary men. Among them as prisoners were the ship's former officers and crew.

A lone figure appeared, proud and silent, on the fire-blackened forecastle. In a spotless blue uniform, red waistcoat, and freshly laundered linen stood John Paul Jones. From the masthead of the captured *Serapis* flew his rattlesnake ensign: "Don't Tread on Me!"

Fighter in the Night

IN EARLY 1780, the king's land and sea forces attacked what was considered to be the "soft underbelly" of the colonies—the South. By May of that year, General Cornwallis reported that he had "put an end to all resistance in South Carolina."

But by late August, Lord Cornwallis knew that he had on his hands an unexpected foe as pesky as the Carolina mosquito and more deadly than the malaria that plagued the British troops. Francis Marion, who was to cause Cornwallis so much grief, was a sharp-faced, little man with a hawk nose and a jutting chin. He came at the British with frightening speed and with devastating power in his sting.

This local militia leader was described in Continental Army reports as "a gentleman of South Carolina, attended by a very few followers, distinguished by small leather caps and the wretchedness of their attire." The description of Colonel Francis Marion and his band continued: "Their number did not exceed twenty men and boys, some white, some black, all mounted, but most of them miserably equipped, their appearance burlesque."

But this little band proved more than a match for the British regulars. Marion and sixteen horsemen appeared out of the steamy wetland one hot summer night and attacked a regiment of redcoats with 160

OVERLEAF:
Second Battle of Freeman's Farm
COURTESY OF THE FORT TICONDEROGA
MUSEUM COLLECTION

American prisoners in their midst. In a brief skirmish, twenty-four of the British soldiers were killed and the rebel captives were set free. Then Marion and his men disappeared into the night.

This was the style of fighting that was soon to drive the British to the point of madness. They hardly ever caught a glimpse of the wispy, little colonel who struck and fled with uncanny skill and speed.

Marion was native to this region of slow-running, mud-laden rivers and black-water swamps. He was a scrawny, wizened veteran of the regional militia, close to fifty years old, but nimble and elusive. Like some night creature of the lowlands, he was safe among the shadows and at home amidst the boggy wilderness. At sundown, when the enemy was retiring to its quarters, Marion and his men were saddling up for a night of forays. By morning he was long gone, leaving behind scenes of chaos.

Marion was a self-reliant field commander who needed no orders from high headquarters. There were, in fact, no such orders. From the Santee River northeast as far as the Peedee, Marion ranged through a country he knew like the calloused palm of his hand. Summer and winter, the partisans camped in the open. They lived off the land on 'possum, yams, and swamp water, operating in outlaw style.

Two British commanders in particular hunted Marion ceaselessly. Colonel Banastre Tarleton and Major James Wemyss were alert to any report or rumor of Marion's whereabouts, but they never succeeded in catching him. In the field, it was Marion's policy to move his trail camp constantly. He could not stop spies from passing to the enemy information about his movements. But by the time the British reached one of his resting places, Marion was elsewhere. On one occasion, British cavalry rode out of their fort to catch him. When they returned, they found that Marion had raided the fort and burned it to the ground.

Major Wemyss vented his fury on the countryside. Frustrated at his inability to capture the guerrillas, the British commander struck savagely at the civilian population. Innocent men were hanged and shot down. Village homes and farmsteads were looted and destroyed. Farm animals were driven into barns which were then put to the torch. Country churches were burned. Forges, gristmills, and looms were wrecked. Crops were set ablaze in the fields and milk cows wantonly slaughtered.

Jean James, whose husband and sons were with Marion, was held prisoner in her home in a scheme to draw the James boys out of hiding. For two days, the redcoats held the woman and her small children—but

Major Wemyss's trap did not work. The irate officer then burned the James home to cinders while Mrs. James and her children looked on.

On September 20, Wemyss reported to Cornwallis: "I have done everything in my power to get Mr. Marion." Then he added, "I have burnt and laid waste to about fifty houses and plantations, mostly belonging to people who have either broke their paroles or oaths of allegiance (to the crown) and are now in arms against us."

Colonel Tarleton had earned a reputation as a brutal, twisted madman on the battlefield, who shot down men who had surrendered and then killed the wounded. At the head of his green-uniformed dragoons, he combed the countryside, swearing that he would not rest until Marion was dead.

He chased the partisan leader for days at a time. But bogs and flooded streams and tangled thickets seemed to rise up before him as he pursued the vanishing Marion. "This damned old fox!" Tarleton exclaimed, giving the swamp fighter his nickname. "The devil himself could not catch him!"

.   .   .

It was here in the South that the Revolution most clearly took on the rabid fury of a civil war with longtime neighbors and kinsmen at war with each other. Hot-tempered loyalties flared on both sides of the conflict. Among the small farmers, tradesmen, and backcountry people, the traditions of liberty were especially strong. On the other hand, many of the aristocrats in the seaboard towns and on the tideland plantations, with strong commercial ties with the mother country, tended to support the British crown. Big slaveholders were extremely suspicious of a Continental Congress that saw all men as "created equal."

A good many in the South were pro-British by custom and habit, and only shifted their allegiance to the American cause in the course of the war. Others leaned toward whichever side seemed to be winning. The struggle between rebels and Tories was bitter, fanatical, and intensely personal.

Marion and his men were aroused to a fighting fury by the merciless treatment which the British troops were dealing out to innocent civilians. They were even more enraged at reports of atrocities by local Tories. Made bold and arrogant by the presence of the British regulars, the friends of Britain were terrorizing the region. To Marion's ears came horror stories about the activities of one Tory in particular, Colonel John Ball.

In late September, Marion gathered his men for an attack on Ball. Having heard how the hated Tories had invaded their homes, the partisans hardly needed urging. The band of horsemen clattered through the canebrake and splashed through the swamps. They caught up with Colonel Ball at Black Mingo Creek. Marion split his small force and attacked the Tory camp at night. As usual, he was assaulting a much larger force than his own. But his men were fired with rage. And in the face of these hot-blooded men, the Tories threw down their guns and ran.

Some of Ball's followers were made prisoners. Marion knew these men and he talked to them earnestly, trying to show them the error of deserting their country in favor of a tyrannous king. Five of them sheepishly admitted they had been misled and agreed to join Marion's band. For all his courage as a fighter, Marion was not a vindictive man. And this was only one of the many occasions on which he showed compassion and fairness.

Marion had witnessed in South Carolina how the British lost the support of a great many of their pro-Tory followers through their own cruelty and arrogance. "Had the British but acted as a wise and magnanimous enemy," Marion told his aides at the campfire one night, "they might easily have recovered the revolted colonies."

On the last day of the year 1780, Marion's men staged an old-fashioned, down-country, hob-raising spree. Their spindly, little commander had been appointed brigadier general. Some men of that rank may have had a wider front of battle to command than did Marion, but there is no record of any that had fewer men to fight with.

Marion could hardly read or write and he had no formal training as a commander. He had made his way up from private to general by promotions on the field of battle. The Swamp Fox took naturally to the art of daring guerrilla warfare and won incredible victories. But his most difficult chore was always the writing of his ungrammatical and misspelled reports of these exploits to higher headquarters.

. . .

An island in the Peedee served as the hideout and rendezvous for Marion and his band. His base camp was on a high, wooded sand ridge that ran the length of Snow's Island. Protecting his rear was a vast stretch of swamp and slough, interlaced with wild bramble hedges and canebrake.

Continental General Nathaniel Greene entered the Carolinas that winter with a rebel army only one-third the size of the British force under Cornwallis. Greene avoided a head-on conflict with the redcoats. And he sought the help of the local partisans for scouting and spying missions. But the American general was a man who put his reliance on regular troops, doubtful that partisan bands could accomplish very

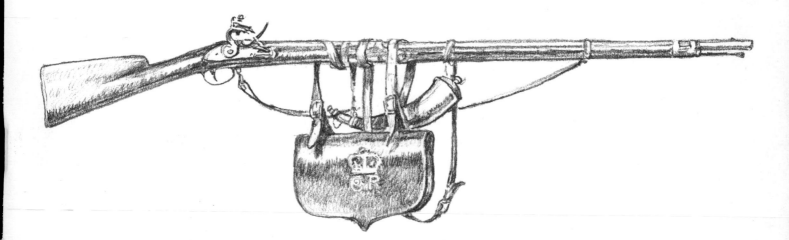

much. Marion and a few others were good officers, Greene commented, "but the people with them just come and go as they please."

In the early spring of 1781, the British made one more determined effort to drive Marion from the Carolina lowlands. They were weary of being outfoxed by the nondescript, little general on his captured horse. The enemy dispatched troopers to scour the countryside in hot pursuit of the elusive rebel leader and his band.

The Swamp Fox now used his full range of wily tactics. He ambushed supply caravans, blocked traffic on the rivers, burned enemy storehouses. Along the Sampit River he fought a series of skirmishes with the main British force under Colonel John Watson.

The partisans made up in speed and deception what they lacked in manpower. Marion and his mounted men nipped at the heels of Watson's infantry. The redcoats were given no rest during the day and little time for sleep at night. Wherever Watson turned, he found his path blocked and beset with danger. Logs lay felled across the narrow

him for exposing himself so carelessly to danger at such a time."

The risk was real. From the massive British fort under rebel siege, the cannons kept up a steady barrage. A belch of fire from one gun, then the next and the next, kept the night alive with noise and terror.

Martin dug hard and deep. The earth was the soldier's refuge. And yet, at any moment, a British cannoneer might touch fire to his weapon and send death whirling toward this trench or that. The diggers were now "a little jealous of our safety," as Martin later wrote, "being without arms and within forty rods of the British trenches."

Martin, a private in the Continental ranks for six years, had been made corporal and now sergeant. He was a volunteer in the sappers and miners, who scored high on hard work and low on survival. They were the "dirt-eaters" of the army, the men who went out on the battlefield with no protection whatever to dig and build safe entrenchments for the rest of the troops.

To the left, at the far end of the wide semicircle of the Continental siege forces, a series of huge bonfires suddenly flared up. Martin could see hundreds of men passing before the blaze. And now the British guns opened up in that direction, concentrating their cannon fire that way for the rest of the night.

Martin chuckled. He knew that the bonfires were a diversion, a scheme to direct British attention away from the trench diggers. The rain was coming hard now, like flying stones. Martin pounded his shovel deeper into the earth, eager to be finished.

To the sergeant, the war had not been continuous fighting. But he recalled that these years had been full of constant and repeated risks. Martin was a bright, robust, spirited, warm-hearted young man who rarely permitted himself to think of death or even danger. Back in 1775 he had enlisted for six months at the age of fifteen, leaving his native village in western Massachusetts.

He had seen action many times in the battles of Long Island, White Plains, and Monmouth. But enemy fire was not the only hazard of war, nor even the greatest. The soldier's ways to death were many. Martin had felt he was dying a score of times—from unfit food and poisoned water, from injuries and fatigue, from deadly fevers and infected wounds, from thirst and starvation, from exposure to blistering sun and shrieking blizzards.

He recalled his time of torment at Valley Forge and "bare feet leaving a track of blood on the frozen ground." But he complained little, even though he wondered "why were we made to suffer so much in so good and just a cause?"

Martin had once returned from a visit home to find that his regiment had left him behind—and alone, Martin had hiked four hundred miles to catch up with his outfit. The sense of duty that had compelled him to carry on "half-starved and three-quarters naked" was something that Martin had felt even when he had first volunteered as a mere boy.

"I collected pretty correct ideas of the contest between this country and the mother country," he recalled. "I was as warm a patriot as the best of them."

October 7. By the light of day, Martin viewed the wide panorama of the Yorktown siege. He was an enlisted man and no expert at military defense. But he was impressed with the might of Corn-

wallis's fort. This was the site the British general had himself chosen as the base from which America would finally be conquered with the large combined army under his command.

In midsummer, Cornwallis had put thousands of soldiers and civilians to work building an impregnable bastion. Three months in construction, the riverside stronghold was a model of classical fortification. It was unnamed, but its builder was probably hoping that in the British America of the future it would be known as "Fort Cornwallis."

England had won almost all its seaport battles in this war, and it seemed unlikely that Cornwallis could lose at Yorktown. Water was the British ally. With this in mind, Cornwallis had built his fort so that it was secured at the rear by the broad expanse of the York River, flowing into Chesapeake Bay, with the open Atlantic just beyond.

A month earlier, in September, French ships had appeared, skirmishing with British men-o'-war in Chesapeake Bay. The clash decided nothing, but the British ships returned to New York for repairs. Cornwallis expected his navy back in force any day now. Meanwhile, the French fleet stood out in the bay. The York River was too shallow for them to bring their guns within range of Yorktown.

As far west and north as Sergeant Joseph Plumb Martin could see, the British fortress was now ringed with American and French troops. At the southern end, all the way to the river's edge, were the Americans. This was the sector across which Martin and his men had helped to build the long trench, the so-called first parallel, for the protection of the attackers. On this day, October 7, every hand was needed to move the artillery into the new emplacements. Teams of oxen tugged at the big guns.

In a little journal which he kept, Martin noted that there had been no rest for him in the night—or in the day. But fatigue was an old and familiar soldier's complaint.

"I have fallen asleep while walking the road," Martin recalled, "and not been sensible of it till I have jostled against someone. And when permitted to stop and have the superlative happiness to roll myself in my blanket and drop down on the ground in the bushes, briars, thorns or thistles, and get an hour or two's sleep, O! how exhilerating."

October 8. This day, the British bombardment thundered cease-

lessly. Martin noted that the Americans had not yet replied with a single shot. Fire, to come at last from the Continental lines, would be no scattered rattle of musketry, no occasional blast from separate artillery pieces. Try as he might, Martin could hardly imagine the full fury of that first massed bombardment discharging down on the British fortress, the earth shuddering, the skies ablaze.

October 9. Tension was now mounting on the Continental side. Every man knew that to take Yorktown the Americans would have to move directly into the British barrage and eventually storm the fortress itself.

October 10. Martin's sappers and miners worked steadily into the late afternoon without a pause. The guns were now all in place. And when Martin said he was hungry, he heard a familiar response, "Find your own."

This strange American army did not ordinarily issue rations to its men. Instead, they were obliged to forage, beg, or filch whatever they could—or else they starved.

Martin had become a master at such skills. Near an abandoned farm, he captured a small pig, "as no owner appeared to be at hand." This provided a satisfying meal of roast pork. Unfortunately, however, the only drinking water thereabouts was from a frog pond where the cavalry horses were also watered. Martin drank the unpalatable stuff, grateful for any water at all.

In the late afternoon, he counted ninety-two cannons, American and French, now ready for action. "All were upon the tiptoe of expectation and impatience to see the signal given to the whole line of batteries, which was to be the hoisting of the American flag," Martin recorded.

Shortly after 5:00 P.M. came the command to fire. The cannoneer who touched off the opening gun was none other than General Washington himself.

"I confess I felt a secret pride swell in my heart," wrote Martin, "when I saw the 'star-spangled banner' waving majestically."

All up and down the American and French lines the boom of cannons resounded louder and louder. From this moment on, these guns were never still. During the next two days and nights, a wide arc of batteries poured havoc on the British fort.

October 13. Siege was the warfare of big guns, and the shelling of Yorktown was a duel of thunderbolts. It required the science of trained artillery commanders and the sweat of cannoneers, hopping frantically to the rapid tempo of "Charge, load, aim, fire!"

For the sappers and miners, now began the dangerous work of moving the line of fire three hundred yards closer to the enemy. The second parallel must be prepared.

That night a mass of strange, antlike creatures crept silently forward from the rebel lines to begin the digging. Squirming and twisting, the trench diggers moved across the bomb craters and debris. They dragged hoes, spades, picks. Many pushed ahead of them bags and baskets full of sand and tied bundles of branches for use in reinforcing the earthworks. They were well within range of the enemy field guns. Near the riverside, they were also menaced by musketry. Here the British had built two small forts or redoubts, which were outside of the main fortification.

All night the men worked. By morning the second parallel was almost ready. To finish the task would mean the storming of the two enemy redoubts.

October 14. By agreement of the commanders, the French were to take Redoubt No. 9 while the Americans assaulted No. 10. On order, the soldiers that night emptied their muskets. No accidental firing of a gun must be allowed to betray the secrecy of this dangerous mission. The bayonet alone would decide the outcome of the fighting.

The two redoubts were star-shaped emplacements for howitzers and mortars, strongly built and ringed with a series of outer defenses. It was the task of the sappers to clear a path through these barriers.

Suddenly came the signal to advance. The tense whisper "Up, up!" was heard all along the ranks. Silently the Americans moved toward Redoubt No. 10. Sergeant Martin, armed with nothing more than an ax, took the lead. He reached the first line of obstruction—stout poles pointed outward, each cut with a slanting stroke that made them sharp as spears. At a signal, Martin's men began to hack at these spiny barricades.

The enemy now opened fire on the attackers with small arms, field pieces, hand grenades. The watchword of the rebel assault was "Rochambeau," the name of the French commander. To Martin's ears it sounded like "Rush on, boys!" And this was the battle cry that now came from the throats of the charging rebels.

The men flung themselves across a ditch, vaulted up over a palisade of sharp-pointed logs. In the redoubt, the fighting was fierce. The sappers, their work finished, crowded on toward the fort. Their officer barred the way. But Martin and his men ignored him. "We will go in!" they shouted, their axes poised. "Then go to the devil!" the lieutenant yelled back and followed them into the furious battle. It was all over in minutes of terrible bloodshed. In Redoubt No. 10, the Hessians and British flung away their arms and pleaded for mercy. It wasn't long before the French captured No. 9.

October 15. The British guns were quiet this day and the Americans wondered what mischief Lord Cornwallis was up to. In reality, British ammunition was running low. The siege had also drained the fort of food and other supplies, and the situation of the defenders was becoming critical. Cornwallis had now begun to lose some of his bravado. Dispatches from New York disclosed that the British fleet, which he had counted on for reinforcements, had run into a series of delays, and it was doubtful that they could leave within the next forty-eight hours.

OVERLEAF:
Moving Farther Westward, 1882
by James Henry Beard
COURTESY OF KENNEDY GALLERIES, INC.

But Cornwallis was a resourceful general who had never surrendered in battle and had no intention of ever doing so. He assured his staff that he had any number of ways out of the trap—and even a few possibilities of turning his present plight into a smashing triumph. As commander of the main British force in America, he held not the slightest doubt that his would be the final victory.

His first counterblow was a raid against the redoubts captured by the rebels. But the British raiders were routed with heavy losses.

October 16. General Cornwallis now busied himself with a plan to escape from the doomed fortress with his army intact. At nightfall he had a fleet of barges ready on the Yorktown docks. His plan was to cross the river to Gloucester and make his way northward to New York. It was a daring scheme that might have worked.

By midnight, the barges made their first ferrying trip. It was just about then that the skies unloosed torrents. The winds rose in a furious squall. Lightning flashes revealed Cornwallis's drenched army, huddled on the banks of the York River. The barges were being tossed about like toys in the rampaging waters. From the British commander came the order to cancel the whole escape operation.

October 17. Sergeant Martin happened to remember that on this date, four years earlier, a whole British army had surrendered at Saratoga. "A rather unlucky day for the British," he mused.

If Martin had owned a spyglass, he might have seen Lord Cornwallis standing at dawn on the battered ramparts of the British fort. The commander stared for a long time at the Yorktown battlefield.

Later that morning a small, red-coated figure suddenly appeared on the wall of the fort. He was a drummer boy, standing alone amid the flying shot and shells, his fierce drumming drowned by the deafening roar of the guns. Gradually the firing subsided. A British officer carrying a white flag now appeared at the side of the drummer, and the two advanced across the broken field of battle.

What could this mean? To Martin in his trench, the war had gone on so long that a simple ending was beyond belief. The battlefield suddenly turned deathly silent, except for the crisp rattle of the drum. The two figures crossed the scarred land to the American lines. A brief note from Cornwallis was handed over. The British general was ready to "settle terms for surrender."

The fighting was at an end.

To Joseph Plumb Martin it all seemed incredible. He had been in the war almost from its beginning; was he at last really seeing its end? With his comrades-in-arms, he had managed to come through years of suffering, just short of death and defeat. And now he was witnessing the most astonishing moment of all—to "come off conquerors at last!"

.   .   .

Perhaps such disbelief was uppermost in the minds of most rebel soldiers as the startling news of Yorktown came to them in America's far-scattered battlefields, forts, camps, and outposts. Few had any notion of the full meaning of the Revolution. Not many had any clear idea that they were in fact creating the first model democratic nation in the modern world. Nor that they had begun the end of the old system of colonialism. They could not foresee that they were setting into motion an experiment in freedom that would continue for hundreds of years.

And yet, many a soldier of the Revolution sensed that he was fighting for some great liberating cause. Such wistful yearnings for freedom may be the very stuff of heroism. If so, perhaps this is what went into the making of Yankee Doodle—the most surprising of victors, the most unlikely of heroes.

"The times that tried men's souls are over," wrote Tom Paine in the last of his *Crisis Papers*. It was he who best summed up the jubilant mood of America's men and women who in liberty's service had found in themselves wellsprings of unsuspected courage.

And Paine caught the spirit in which they now turned to the ways of peace and nation-building. "It would be a circumstance ever to be lamented and never to be forgotten," he wrote, "were a single blot, from any cause whatever, to fall on a revolution which to the end of time must be an honor to an age that accomplished it; and which has contributed more to enlighten the world and diffuse a spirit of freedom and liberality among mankind than any human event that ever preceded it."

93

PRINTED IN U.S.A.

Continued from inside of front cover

and Howard Pyle. Complementing these are
black and white line drawings by the well-
known illustrator Lorence Bjorklund.

Thus it is through an exciting combination
of vivid writing and dramatic illustrations that
new life is brought to this period in America's
history, enabling the reader to experience the
birth of a nation.

ABOUT THE AUTHOR . . .

Author of outstanding books for children and
young adults, S. Carl Hirsch now follows his
FAMOUS AMERICAN INDIANS OF THE PLAINS
with FAMOUS AMERICAN REVOLUTIONARY WAR
HEROES. A well-established writer, the high
quality of his work has often been recognized
and he is the recipient of many awards—among
them two Thomas Alva Edison Awards, the
Clara Ingraham Judson Award, and the Jane
Addams Award.

ABOUT THE ILLUSTRATOR . . .

Long interested in American history, Lorence
Bjorklund has illustrated three other titles in
Rand McNally's *"Famous American"* series—
FAMOUS AMERICAN INDIANS OF THE PLAINS,
FAMOUS AMERICAN EXPLORERS, and FAMOUS
AMERICAN TRAILS. Much of the research for
FAMOUS AMERICAN REVOLUTIONARY WAR
HEROES was done by Mr. Bjorklund at West
Point where he was able to sketch actual arti-
facts dating to the revolutionary period.

CANADA

SUPERIOR

L. HURON

MICHIGAN

SIN

L. MICHIGAN

WISCONSIN

ILLINOIS

MAINE

VT.

N.H.

L. ONTARIO

NEW YORK

Hudson River

MASS.

CONN.

R.I.

★ Saratoga

Lexington

Bunker Hill

INDIANA

OHIO

L. ERIE

White Plains ★

Princeton ★

Delaware

□ Manhattan

Long Island ★

Trenton

Monmouth

Valley Forge □

N.J.

• Philadelphia

DEL.

MD.

WEST

VIRGINIA

□ Vincennes

Ohio River

Yorktown ★

VIRGINIA

Chesapeake

Bay

□ Kaskaskia

KENTUCKY

NORTH CAROLINA

TENNESSEE

SOUTH

CAROLINA

ATLANTIC OCEAN

MISSISSIPPI

ALABAMA

GEORGIA

FLORIDA

G OF MEXICO

LEGEND

— Original 13 Colonies'
Prewar Boundary *

★ Battle Sites

* Note: The original 13 colonies
are labeled in blue. Other states
indicated on the map are for
present-day orientation.